My Soul Is a Witness

My Soul Is a Witness

The Message of the Spirituals in Word and Song

Marsha Hansen

Augsburg Books

MINNEAPOLIS

Library of Congress Cataloging-in-Publication Data
Hansen, Marsha, 1952-
   My soul is a witness! : the message of the spirituals in word and song
 / Marsha Hansen.
     p. cm.
   Includes bibliographical references and index.
   ISBN 0-8066-5285-3 (jacketed hardcover with CD : alk. paper)
   1. Spirituals (Songs)—History and criticism. I. Title.
 ML3556.H26 2006
 782.25'3—dc22   2006007270

Cover design by Charles Brock, The DesignWorks Group; Cover photo © LaShun Beal, "Soulful Flight." Used by permission.
Book design by Michelle L. N. Cook

For recording credits, see page 127.

This book is dedicated to the memory of my beloved parents,
Kirby L. Robinson and Mary Alice Robinson.

The CD is dedicated to the memory of Joseph G. Jacques.

Acknowledgments

I gratefully acknowledge the support and help of my husband, Rodney Hansen, and our children, Jordan, Joel, and Alex in writing this book. I also thank Keith and Patti Richards for their unflagging support and encouragement in completing the companion CD.

I offer special thanks to veteran record producer, Rob Fraboni, who gathered together many of the artists who perform on the *My Soul Is a Witness* CD, and to Scott Tunseth at Augsburg Fortress, Publishers, for his patient guidance. Their vision and dedication helped to bring this project to fruition.

I deeply appreciate advice from my friend, Peter Huchthausen, who has been a faithful mentor, generous in sharing his insights as a professional writer.

Lastly, I thank my beloved former professor, Dr. Roy John Enquist, who has my gratitude not only for teaching me in the classroom, but for being one of those persons who, through his own example, equipped me to be a person of faith.

Contents

Introduction

I find an exquisite joy in sharing God's radiant presence through song, and I especially love singing the sacred songs of my African American ancestors. The historic songs known variously as Negro spirituals, or African American spirituals, are very personal in intent and in content. They convey ageless messages of faith and of life's experiences laid bare. As is poignantly true with some other musical forms, the rhythms, tunes, and poetry of spirituals overcome the limitations of language and of human understanding in ways that transcend words, time, place, and culture. This is music that is at once culturally rich, yet totally inclusive. Perhaps the simple truth is that all good music somehow serves to breach existential loneliness and bring segments of humanity together in closer communion. Certainly, the particular music that originated among enslaved Africans and their progeny has powerfully linked human beings all over the world to each other and to the divine.

I often sing my songs in a concert setting. Sometimes when I glimpse the faces of my audiences, I see private moments of reflection at which I am privileged to be present; so, even as a soloist, I am aware that music is a jointly creative undertaking.

For me, there is a lifting up, a sense of reaching beyond my own abilities and talents to include the faith and longings that the accompanists and the listeners bring to the experience. There is a comfort and a familiarity in the music that I sing, but I believe the deeper reason that the African American spirituals in my repertoire continue to speak to people from all walks of life is that they are songs of universal truth. The longing behind the plaintive cry sung in "Give Me Jesus" is in the hearts of people everywhere who are seeking God. Whoever first sang, "My Soul Is a Witness for My Lord," was speaking for me. This is my truth, but it is not mine alone. It is the same truth that an anonymous enslaved person voiced in the American South in the days before freedom. It is the same truth that the psalmist declared when he wrote that even the waters clap for joy in the presence of God.

Over time, I have discovered that the appeal of the old spirituals is very much the same appeal as that of the biblical Psalms. There are distinct reasons for making this claim. One may consider for instance, that the belief in and longing for the presence of the holy are at the core of both poetic forms. Furthermore, the longing for purpose and relationship are clear in each. Just as the psalmist wrote of deep meditation, of searching for God and desiring his companionship, the composers of spirituals also spoke of wanting and needing God, and of stealing away to be with him. Each form emphasizes concerns about brotherhood, about self understanding, about interacting with other people in intentional and righteous ways, and always about living as though indeed there is a God who sees.

Both psalms and spirituals originated among peoples who had suffered and borne the bitterness of enslavement and who had held on to the hope of the deliverance through divine agency. In spirituals, the weight of sufferings and longings are often captured in more than just words. The intonation of a moan sometimes speaks directly to the heart, and the rich timbre of a hum can convey as much meaning or depth of emotion as the most carefully worded speech. Still, as with many of the psalms, spirituals incorporate the power of story in the search for the holy truth. This desire to capture the truth is what makes storytelling enduring and necessary. When good, insightful stories are set to music, they become profoundly memorable. This is one key to the enduring life of Negro spirituals. In fact, it has been claimed that one can make a journey through the scriptural stories, from Genesis to Revelation, by listening to spirituals. Certain themes are more emphasized than others, but most Old and New Testament events and teachings are at least alluded to somewhere in the great body of spirituals that exists.

Not surprisingly, the structure of the music of Africa is ideally suited to bring the heart of story to all people. African singing is typically passionate, repetitive, rhythmic, harmonically rich, and filled with nuances of dynamic interest ranging from quiet passages to bursts of joyous, rising crescendo. Minor keys are regularly relied upon to add texture and depth to the music.

In the same way, there are certain cultural hallmarks that especially distinguish African American vocal music. Syncopation and antiphonal elements are important cultural elements of our singing, arranging and understanding song. Vocal slides, or glissandi, done in characteristically unique cultural ways are typical and essential to emphasizing both mood and message of the music.

The combination of African and African American musical structures can be found in the wealth of spirituals that the world has inherited. The result is songs that are rich in sacred story, musical interpretation, and personal reflection.

Why write a book about spirituals? What more is there to say about them given the fact that there has long been an interest in them as more than simply a musical form? African American or Negro spirituals have already been written about by sociologists, historians, ethnomusicologists and other scholars interested in cataloging and preserving individual songs. People have sought to trace the importance of this music as an element of worship and a method of social expression. Others have sought to determine the complex cultural roots of the music and explore its unique characteristics as a musical form. Yet, there remains much to be gleaned from our historic African American religious music.

Originating in the earliest days of American slavery and continuing to develop in post-Civil War America, certain spirituals, such as "Let Us Break Bread Together," are routinely found in hymnals as standard Christian anthems; yet these songs were sung first in the camp meetings of the slaves as they heard and believed together that what the Lord had done for others, he would do for them.

Who could imagine better what it was like to be in a lion's den than the people who daily had their backs whipped and their children stolen and their dignity stripped away at the merest whim? It is easy to draw parallels. If the Lord could close the hungry mouths of the beasts set to devour Daniel, could he not deliver the enslaved from their troubles and cares? "Didn't My Lord Deliver Daniel?" tells not only of Daniel's safety in the arms of the Lord, but it also tells of the delivery of Jonah from the belly of the whale and of the three Hebrew children who were cast into the fiery furnace by the angry king Nebuchadnezzar. These biblical characters were people with troubles so heavy that no ordinary power could possibly save them, yet all were delivered. In the case of Daniel and of the three Hebrew children, the oppressors were changed men as well. The song becomes a tool of reflection as similar biblical stories are grouped together for consideration. It is as if the slaves said among themselves, "Look at all these instances of saving grace and intervention. The same God is our God, too."

The majesty and saving power of God came through so clearly to the enslaved Africans in America that they were able to capture these ideas in song and proclaim the truth of God's might and love for those God calls his own. That an oppressed people sang these truths reveals a hope and a glory and a comfort that God in his grace had made possible.

Collectively then, spirituals represent a repository of profound theological and religious philosophical reflection that is possible to overlook if this body of songs is simply viewed as folk music limited by contexts of time and circumstance. Likewise, if the texts of the songs are viewed only as literal interpretations of biblical Scripture or events, much of the insight of the composers is missed.

In this book you will find a discussion centering on the changes in religious focus and understanding that Christianity engendered for people of African descent. There is also an exploration of how the people themselves found expression for their interior and practical needs through this new religion. Finally, this book addresses whether a people can legitimately and authentically embrace a religion espoused by their oppressors. In each case, the voice of the people who wrote the songs speaks. The text of the spirituals or oratory from this period in history provide the basis for all claims in this book.

Letting the texts speak for themselves is extremely important and has not always been done. In 1964 E. Franklin Frazier published *The Negro Church in America* in which spirituals and gospel music were described in derisive language. This book was received with critical acclaim and is still referenced today as a pivotal sociological treatment of the black religious experience in America. It is an important book, but upon close reading, it must be observed that the book is hostile to Christianity in general. While recognizing the history of the "Negro church" as an instrument of social cohesion, it blatantly denounces the institutional church as a stumbling block to intellectual and social progress. Frazier writes that "The Negro church and Negro religion have cast a shadow over the entire intellectual life of Negroes and have been responsible for the so-called backwardness of American Negroes. . . . It is only as a few Negro individuals have been able to escape from the stifling domination of the church that they have been able to develop intellectually and in the field of art."[1]

The Negro Church in America does precisely the type of thing that it accuses the anti-intellectual element of the church of doing, which is to offer a pitying and condescending view of the religious traditions that originated among illiterate adherents of Christianity. The rich religious legacy of enslaved African American people is depicted as wholly derivative and unimaginative. The God of the Bible is written of as "the god of the white man." From a strictly sociological point of view, perhaps such interpretations are understandable. The social scientist writes as if there is no God, but only "the god of . . ." as a strictly utilitarian human construct. Where African Americans were concerned, Frazier viewed Christianity primarily as a tool of accommodation, and as a means of appropriating an inferior self-concept.

The Christian theologian and the believer have a different view of religious reality. They understand that there are two aspects to the church, the very fallible human social institution with its failures and triumphs, and also the divine, active spiritual body that binds and inspires. Rather than denounce the faith statements of illiterate or semi-literate people as "pathetic associations with which the faith and piety of many generations have invested the familiar words (of the Bible),"[2] one has the choice to honor the faith and piety of the generations as authentic participation in the mystical body of Christ. I choose to approach my study of sacred African American folk music from this point of view.

My Soul Is a Witness is unabashedly written from a Christian viewpoint. In this book, I intend to illumine not only some of the historical, but the theological underpinnings of African American spirituals.

In 1945, Howard Thurman published a remarkable book on Negro spirituals that is filled with grace and insight and is as relevant today as when it first appeared. I view his book, *Deep River,* as the antecedent of this current volume. Mine is an effort to continue the conversation Thurman began on the deeper messages of the religious folk music the world first called Negro spirituals.

A Word about the Recording

Like families everywhere, when my family gathers, we like to eat good food, listen to good music, and tell stories. I am blessed to have talented musicians on both sides of my family, and remarkably blessed to have been able to record some music at a family gathering with my brother-in-law, Keith Richards. Many of the songs on this CD are the spontaneous result of some evenings spent together with friends in the comfort of a home setting, where we enjoyed talking about the roots of sacred African American music. The first seven songs are actual at-home recordings, done between meals, with lots of laughter and more serious moments of reflection. The music is authentic and highly representative of the folk roots of the African American spiritual, even if most of the performers also happen to be professional rock musicians.

Our good friend and producer, Rob Fraboni, set things up for us to record our music and invited some old friends to come and join our home session. Babi Floyd, Blondie

Chaplin, George Receli, Nick Tremulus, Paul Nowinski, Chuck Leavell, Steven Barber, and John Pirruccello joined with Keith Richards, my daughter Jordan Hansen, and me to interpret old songs in ways that perfectly fit the original mood and message of each one. The familiar tunes are recognizable beneath the innovative arrangements, and the soulful feel of the songs is strongly there in the music recorded at the Richards' home.

The rest of the more traditional arrangements of songs on the CD are deeply felt as well, and are performed in my typical concert style with my dear friend and frequent accompanist, Joyce Perez, at the piano. We had a wonderful time in San Diego where Joyce got her first taste of a recording studio. Jordan and I, joined by bass Walt Gustafson, enjoyed every moment singing the songs that have been familiar to us for many years. Later on, Paul Nowinski joined us back on the East Coast and added his marvelous stringed instruments for us.

I hope you enjoy listening to the music and reading the book *My Soul Is a Witness.* Both are presented with great love and deep respect for the experiences that gave rise to African American spirituals.

Walking the Walk

It is not unusual for me to open a concert with "I Want Jesus to Walk with Me." I offer it as a prayer and a testimony. It speaks to a deep need for, a faith in, and a recognition of who Jesus is. Some may simply think of this as a familiar, powerful hymn without realizing that it is in fact an African American spiritual, originating among the disenfranchised in the antebellum South. What is moving about this song is the depth of religious expression as it views the individual person in relationship to Jesus. There is a certainty, a taking for granted, that such a relationship can exist. It is striking that this certainty developed among a people to whom Christianity had been a foreign religion, and to whom Christianity was often presented in a distorted form to preserve the institution of slavery. Yet, in the words of the song, Jesus emerges not as the cultural captive of any one group of people, but as the promise of salvation to all believers and as the foundation of liberation in this life.

The lyrics are:

I Want Jesus to Walk with Me

I want Jesus to walk with me.

I want Jesus to walk with me.

All along my pilgrim journey,

Oh Lord, I want Jesus to walk with me.

In my trials, Lord walk with me.

In my trials, Lord walk with me.

When my heart is almost breaking,

Oh Lord, I want Jesus to walk with me.

When I'm in trouble, Lord walk with me.

When I'm in trouble, Lord walk with me.

When my head is bowed down in sorrow,

Oh Lord, I want Jesus to walk with me.

Walk with me, Lord.

Walk with me.

Walk with me, Lord.

Walk with me.

All along my pilgrim journey,

Oh, Lord, I want Jesus to walk with me.

Two things are immediately apparent in this song: whoever composed the song looked at life as a journey and each element in the idea of a "pilgrim journey" is important. A pilgrim is one specifically on a faith quest, so we can understand that in this song, life is viewed as purposeful. There are choices to be made and a destination to be gained. Both spiritual and material dimensions of life are considered. The notion of the journey further seems to convey, that no matter how troubled life is, an individual does not have travel the path alone. There is one who can be present as a companion and helper all the way. This is Jesus.

Who is Jesus, and who is this Lord? What is his connection to human beings? Who among us merits his ministrations? What is my response to him? How did the enslaved person come to know of him?

The affirmation in this song is that through Jesus we encounter a God who bends to humanity and meets us in our needs, humblest circumstances not withstanding. He is a God who sees worth in those he has created and calls them friends. He is a God who is willing to dwell with us. There is not one of us who merits his attention, but through his grace and mercy, each of us receives his attention. "Oh Lord, I want Jesus to walk with me."

Who am "I" in this song? I am a pilgrim, a created person with a purpose. I do not live in an impersonal universe, though I may live with injustice and imbalance and unanswered questions. I have trials and heartbreak and pain to face, but I also have a destination and an inward assurance that God cares and *that* is what matters and gives meaning to each of my moments. God is the light that penetrates my deepest darkness.

How could a person in miserable slavery arrive at such beliefs? It is important to note that Christianity was a new religion to the Africans who were forced into slavery. It represented a radical departure from some religious essentials in which the African people had been grounded in their own cultures. In Africa, one derived a sense of oneself as rooted in history with strong ties to the past. Myths abounded to explain the natural world, and objects were commonly viewed as imbued with spirits, either benign or malevolent. Typically, animists or pantheists, the African person's religious orientation was toward the past, toward the ancestor, toward the origin of things, toward one's place in the physical world relative to other beings and things.

While the idea of one creator was not an unfamiliar concept to Africans, there was a diverse pantheon of deities to represent divine powers and attributes. This is quite different than monotheism.

Further distinctions are that the present and future orientation of Christianity, the hope for things to come, the notion of a savior and a loving God whom one could address as "Father" represented new perspectives. The prevailing religious philosophies and beliefs that took root and flourished among enslaved Africans in America in light of the two conflicting cosmological positions, along with the attempt by slaveholders to present a truncated, distorted, self-serving version of Christianity are extremely profound. Oh, Lord, I want Jesus.

What was the slave experience like? Consider that the systematic and callous stripping away of culture and any sense of unity among the West African people who found themselves victimized by European slave trade was vital to the plans of the slave trader and slave holder. If connections based on language, religion, custom, family, or village could be broken, then a more docile, compliant chattel would be the result. In other words, break the bonds and break the spirit and bend the will.

Ibo, Ashanti, and other West African people steeped in traditions centuries old suddenly found themselves stranded in a strange land in horrific bondage. They may have been war captives sold to Europeans by rival chieftains or tribal people. They may have been caught in raids on villages. They may have been hunted specifically to meet the greed of the slave trade. These certainly were not all people coming from idyllic lives. Prior to enslavement they were subject to the same kinds of social conflicts and civil abuses and vagaries of class structures and survival issues that people in other societies faced. Their strengths in their homelands, lay in family, in familiarity of the landscape, in familiar customs, folkways, and beliefs. Now stripped of these, what was available for them in which to anchor hope and plans and identity as human beings?

Simone Weil writes that "One cannot lose more than the slave loses, he loses all inner life. He only retrieves a little if there should arise an opportunity to change his destiny."[1] I believe this loss of inner life is only true when the enslaved person "bends with the remover to remove" his sense of his humanity. When persons accept their own enslavement as part of the natural order, that is when they become servile objects. That is when they participate in abdicating their own humanity. In fact, despite all attempts to humiliate and dehumanize Black persons enslaved in America, there grew a corporate strength and identity and a strong sense of an inner life that was passed on to the generations through the beliefs reflected in spirituals and religious rhetoric. Today's sense of Black American unity, community, and faith originated among people who did not renounce their own humanity. A thinking and communicating people who found strength by the grace of God forged an identity in a foreign land and have seen their lives of faith influence a nation and the world.

The brutality of slavery in America and throughout the Caribbean cannot be overstated. Not only were fundamental human rights denied, and bodies and minds tortured, but the very idea that Africans were fully human was called into question, with some Whites publicly proclaiming that Black people had no souls. When Christianity was presented to the enslaved, entire passages of Scripture were either conveniently omitted or twisted to validate slavery. One example is in the case of the Exodus story. This was either not presented at all, or presented in a version that has Moses leading the children of Israel back to Pharaoh.

In a speech given by Frederick Douglass at Finsbury Chapel, Moorfields, England, May 12, 1846, the evils of slavery for the bondsman as well as the slaveholder are so eloquently and incisively depicted as to leave no one insensible to the moral bankruptcy or brutality of the system. Douglass, the escaped son of a slave and brother to four slaves, felt a tremendous burden to expend his last ounce of energy to expose and destroy this institution. In this speech, Douglass so indicts the practice of religion in the American South and its upholding of the institution of slavery, that the Southerner's version of Christianity appears corrupt, distorted, truncated, and bastardized so as to be unrecognizable as Christianity. Conversely, he so passionately and with such inspired clarity defends his understanding of the true cause of Christ, that his words stand as a creedal statement.

> I love the religion of our blessed Savior. I love that religion that comes from above, in "the wisdom of God, which is first pure, then peaceable, gentle, and easy to be entreated, full of mercy and good fruits, without partiality and without hypocrisy." I love that religion that sends its votaries to bind up the wounds of him who has fallen among thieves. I love that religion that makes it the duty of its disciples to visit the fatherless and the widow in their affliction. I love that religion that is based upon the glorious principle, of love to God and love to man; which makes its followers do unto others as they themselves would be

done by. If you demand liberty yourself, it says, grant it to your neighbors. If you claim a right to think for yourself, it says, allow your neighbors the same right. It is because I love this religion that I hate the slaveholding, the woman-whipping, the mind-darkening, the soul-destroying religion that exists in the southern states of America. It is because I regard the one as good, pure, and holy, that I cannot but regard the other as bad, corrupt, and wicked. Loving the one I must hate the other; holding to the one I must reject the other.[2]

Oh, Lord, I want Jesus.

Frederick Douglass understood Christianity not as a human construct but as a religion originating with God. He understood there to be a cost to discipleship. He understood there to be no partiality and no hypocrisy in this pure religion. He understood there to be a call to decisive action out of love for God and humanity. These understandings are bold in both their social and theological implications. Socially, they mean that good will cannot be restricted only to those one esteems or with whom one is in agreement. Theologically, they mean that grace is totally inclusive. A basis for understanding social justice from a Christ-like stance is laid out in Douglass's speech. This profound understanding permeates much of the music of this period.

Through the efforts of devout Christian persons and the agency of the Holy Spirit, the living Christ became known to the captives. Unlike Simone Weil's spiritually eviscerated persons, many of the enslaved African persons embraced Christ and claimed him, and developed an authentic self-awareness in relationship to Jesus that empowered them rather than stripped them of humanity. This was despite the oppressive intentions of those who sought to keep them in darkness and bondage. In Christ Jesus there was found a friend of unending devotion. The suffering servant, the man of sorrows, the King of Glory, the truth and the life upheld the enslaved and walked in their plight with them. Oh, Lord, I want Jesus.

Jesus' declaration, "I have called you friends," is possibly the best news of the good news. To have been called into friendship with God, to understand this relationship as the primary pur- pose of creation, to be included in the holy fellowship of friends of Christ, is and was beyond measure in meaning. The awareness of having been called and included not as a slave or a servant, but as a friend, supplies such a sense of spiritual fortitude that adver- sities take on a transitory reality that cannot displace hope.

I do not mean to dismiss suffering and adversity. Human suffering remains one of the most troubling dilemmas of faith that anyone can encounter. Indeed, the biblical book of Job highlights suffering as a dilemma of faith, and the character Job is important in African American self-understanding. Still, the book of Job leaves as many questions about suffering unanswered and unresolved as it raises, but we are given profound insight on how we can face our suffering, if not understand it.

The enslaved African could easily identify with this man named Job. He was a righteous man, a desert prince, a loving father, a faithful friend, and a devoted servant of God. In one catastrophic day he loses his herds and his servants to theft and death. His earthly wealth is gone. He might have recovered eventually from these tragic calamities, but in these same evil moments all ten of his beloved children are claimed by death. If we are to understand the love that God demonstrates toward us in giving up his only begotten son to die on a cross, we have to understand the magnitude of Job's loss at the deaths of his ten begotten children. This is an immense tragedy creating untold sorrow in a father's heart, be he prince or slave. It calls for our deepest compassion even today. But this was not the end of Job's troubles. He was stricken by disgusting diseases that made him a pariah in his day. He was covered in boils, and worms ate at his flesh. People recoiled from him in horror. Tragically adding to his burdens, his friends came to him and, under the guise of condolence, blamed him for his conditions. In their own need to find an explanation for human tragedy, they turned to the expediency of blaming the sufferer. "It must be your fault," they said. "It must."

There are some powerful lessons in Job, if not explanations of human suffering. In the reviled man Job, there was that which clung to life. When he had lost his goods and family, been deserted by his friends, horribly stricken in his flesh, attacked and brought low in every way, his spirit still clung to life.

What was there driving this affirmation of life? Even though Job prayed for death, he did not destroy himself, and he clearly yearned for meaning and purpose and relationship. Out of his cruel suffering and in answer to his tormentors and to himself, he cried, "For I know that my Redeemer lives, and that he will at last stand upon the earth; and after my skin has been thus destroyed, then in my flesh I shall see God, whom I shall see on my side, and my eyes shall behold, and not another. My heart faints within me!" (Job 19: 25-27). This is the distillation of pure hope. This is the recognition and insistence from within that man is more than flesh. The lessons in Job are about life and hope, even in the light of overwhelming disaster and sorrow. They are about the vast gulf between man's ways and God's ways. Job shores us up in our belief that there is more to this experience of being a human being than these days we spend on the earth. His motivation to continue to care is his hope and belief that there is a plan and an answer: "I know that my redeemer lives . . ." Whatever gift there was in Job that equipped him to believe is present in us also. And we are further equipped by the blessing of knowing Jesus by name.

My belief is that the African American slaves were like Job in that they experienced this Redeemer who calls us friends and takes away the power of the adversary and of those eager to blame the sufferer. The slaves' plight brought the meaning of Jesus' words into sharp focus. Here were people who knew in a very direct way what it meant to be reviled, scorned, abused, and misused. To be servants, not in a voluntary, loving capacity but in the mean circumstances of brute slavery, was their constant reality. To know that they not only had little power over their own lives, but could not offer even basic security or protection to their children was a source of heartbreak. To face such a life of hardship daily, and yet to have a certainty that God himself cherished each of them and his relationship with them, provided a spiritual core that gave life value and a spiritual armor that provided remarkable resilience. Eventually, this foundation of faith was instrumental in breaking the chains of slavery. Inspired persons such as Frederick Douglass, Sojourner Truth, Harriet Tubman, and others shed light on the evils of the institution through their courageous words, faith, and actions. Strikingly, these liberators identified themselves as Christians. But even for other persons who remained enslaved for their entire lifetimes, some sense of inner liberation and self-realization could occur based on identity as a friend of Jesus. Oh, Lord, I want Jesus.

> You are my friends if you do what I command you. No longer do I call you servants, for the servant does not know what his master is doing; but I have called you friends, for all that I have heard from my Father I have made known to you. . . . This, I command you, to love one another.
> —John 15:15, 17, RSV

Make me to know thy ways, O Lord:

teach me thy paths,

Lead me in thy truth, and teach me,

for thou art the God of my salvation:

for thee I wait all the day long.

Be mindful of thy mercy, O Lord,

and of thy steadfast love,

for they have been of old.

Remember not the sins of my youth,

or of my transgressions;

according to thcy stcadfast love rcmcmbcr mc,

for thy goodness sake, O Lord!

Good and upright is the Lord:

therefore he instructs sinners in the way.

He leads the humble in what is right,

and teaches the humble his way.

All the paths of the Lord are

steadfast love and faithfulness,

 for those who keep his covenant

and his testimonies.

Psalm 25:4-10, RSV

Songs of Resistance and Protest

African American spirituals take us far beyond mere pathos. They show definite concerns about the human condition; about meaning and purpose; about ultimate meaning; about social justice and social structure; about the natures of God and man; about sin, death, salvation, and grace; and about the role and place of Jesus and Christianity. What does it mean to be human, both in the sense of being a unique individual and being part of the community of human beings? How does one make the emotional and spiritual connections necessary to give meaning to existence, particularly under the forces of harsh oppression? What does it mean to hope? Where is there freedom? These are the questions reflected in this music, and questions about freedom are the core questions.

Perhaps freedom is the only real basis for some ultimate state of being. Our actions as human beings have more apparent meaning when there is choice in their execution. The imposition of external forces certainly shapes all of our lives, whether we have the illusion of power or a sense of powerlessness. It is not until we despair of asking questions that our lives lose meaning and all sense of freedom departs from us. Freedom and all of its implicit responsibility and glory underlies the quest for meaning in life. This is an essential notion that will be developed further in the discussion of the content of spirituals.

Embedded in African American spirituals such as "Nobody Knows the Trouble I've Seen," "Oh, Freedom," "Give Me Jesus," "Listen to the Lambs," and "Wasn't That a Wide River?" are some archetypal questions. They are the same implicit questions that all humanity asks. Is there any grief or dark despair so impenetrable that God cannot reach us there? Is there a disappointment so crushing, a pain so unbearable, that God is unable or unwilling to bear it for us? Are our faith stories just delusions? Are our hopes really empty, meaningless last attempts at denial? Are we each at last simply alone in a merciless and impersonal universe? Are we born to suffer, die, and be forgotten?

Universally, we ask these questions. The answers depend on who God is. Indeed, even more basically, the answers depend on if there is a God. Supposing that there is a God, the answers depend on the nature of God and on the activities and thoughts and plans of God. If there is a God, and if he is concerned with human activity, then the answers also depend on our responses to him and our understanding of how he approaches us.

Throughout the existence of humanity, we have conspired as cultures to explain things. As humans we try to offer explanations for everything that we can conceive of or apprehend in any way. Our myths and poems and stories and music and rituals and religions and sciences all result from this corporate attempt to know. The experience of gathering together to explain their suffering and give voice to their hopes resulted in African American slaves identifying themselves and answering these questions as theists, people who said yes to the existence of God. They identified themselves as recipients of grace, as beneficiaries of God's redemptive love, as participants and inheritors of God's kingdom, and as rebellious enough to ask the questions that people seeking God ask.

Of course, one does not find this formal language, but the thoughts are eloquently and radically presented in the texts of spirituals and slave journals and other authenticated historical sources, as well as in the stories I have gathered firsthand (my own grandfather was born in 1864, during the Civil War in DeSoto County, Mississippi.). There is no need to apologize for the lack of formal language. People can speak the truth by whatever means are available to them.

The song, "Oh, Freedom" is the quintessential protest song. It developed among a group of slaves who saw their situation as such a violation of humankind's purpose that death was preferable. There is in fact a story of a group of slaves who joined arms and marched into the sea to their deaths while singing these words:

Oh, Freedom
Oh, Freedom,
Oh, Freedom,
And before I'd be a slave
I'd be buried in my grave
And go home to my Lord and be free

This is a song that I sing with great reverence and with every attempt to convey in just the two words, "Oh, Freedom" the desire that comes from the heart to live to serve God and others as a free being. To serve others as a sister, not as a thing; to be of service because I choose to be, not because I am coerced, to participate in service to one another, because each of us is created by God, and have a home with him.

Even though it advocates resisting slavery to the point of suicide, "Oh, Freedom" is not advocating death. It is a serious, sad, somber song, but not the song of a broken people. It is the song of a people who recognize their own humanity in the context of faith and values. It is the song of a people who came to understand that their labor and their thoughts and their bodies and their children were their own. They recognized themselves as beings created in the image of God and they prized freedom as a necessary condition for being able to participate fully in God's plan for humanity.

Of course, African Americans were met with arguments from persons claiming that slavery was in fact sanctioned in the Bible. One still hears this argument today. It is true that slavery, as a social fact, is acknowledged in the Bible, yet it is always as Chrysostom, great preacher and Doctor of the Church who lived during the fourth and into the fifth century proclaimed, the result of the sins of avarice, envy, and insatiability. St. Augustine, in *The City of God,* concluded that "[God] did not intend that His rational creature, who was made in His image, should have dominion over anything but the irrational creation—not man over man, but man over beasts." In an 1826 speech, Venezuelan liberator, Simon Bolivar declared that "Slavery is the negation of all law . . . this greatest assault on the dignity of man. I ask you: a man owning another man! A man, an object! One in the image of God yoked like an animal!"

I confess that I have an immediate inner need to protest social structures in which justice and human worth are not fundamental pillars. And because St. Paul's writings urging slaves to obey their masters and masters to treat their slaves fairly have been quoted to uphold the institution of slavery, the same impetus to protest compels me to address his words.

I do not believe that endorsement of slavery was ever St. Paul's purpose. In fact, endorsing slavery is in conflict with his purpose, and when we consider the authority and import given to Scripture as opposed to other historical documents, it is critical to look closely at Paul's meanings. To an even greater extent, it is essential that we look at the whole body of Scripture to discern God's will for our lives. This authority is for all time. We look to the truths of Scripture as eternal. Because so much of Christian practice is based on Pauline writings, I think the passages in Ephesians 6:5-9 and Colossians 3:22-4:1 that treat the master/slave relationship have to be directly addressed. The Ephesians passage reads as follows:

Slaves, obey your earthly masters with respect and fear, and with sincerity of heart, just as you would obey Christ. Obey them not only to win their favor when their eye is on you, but like slaves of Christ, doing the will of God from your heart. Serve wholeheartedly, as if you were serving the Lord, not men, because you know that the Lord will reward everyone for whatever good he does, whether slave or free. And masters, treat your slaves in the same way. Do not threaten them, since you know that he who is both their Master and yours is in heaven, and there is no favoritism with him. (NIV)

It is a serious misapplication of these important verses to interpret them as upholding an evil institution, which is what slavery is. The very fact that Paul's addresses to slaves and masters are juxtaposed next to verses dealing with family relationships seems problematic, but this is explicable. First, Paul has addressed husbands and wives, then parents and children. The husband and wife relationship is a covenanted relationship ordained by God. The parent and child relationship is a blood tie. We accept both of these as natural relationships, and Paul is writing about behavior within relationships. Slavery in Rome was widespread in his day and there were slaves in the earliest

Christian congregations. Throughout Scripture, however, slavery is presented as a bitter yoke, always the result of conflict, greed, and enmity. One cannot imagine Moses being satisfied if only Pharaoh would agree to cultivate the behavior among masters and slaves in Egypt that Paul describes. God's message to Pharaoh was "Let my people go, or else . . ." Clear message.

We need to understand that Paul is addressing a reality of his day when he speaks to masters and slaves. Paul certainly knew his history and Scripture. He was a learned man and a Roman citizen. In his day, the Roman Empire was heavily populated by slaves as a result of many conquests. The might and power of Rome was recognized and feared. People who had fallen subject to Rome knew the weight and reach of Roman tyranny and oppression. It is a topic of protest throughout the New Testament. Unscrupulous tax collectors, oppressive foreign governors such as Pontius Pilate, a formidable coercive military force, and rampant slavery were common realities throughout the empire. None of these met any ideal.

As in all of his epistles, Paul sought to address relationships and behaviors among members of Christian congregations as they sought changes in their lives in contrast to the practices surrounding them. Paul expected the imminent return of

Christ and thus he was not addressing social justice or seeking broad social change when he spoke to masters and slaves. Paul was trying to change hearts. He urgently sought the transformation of the inner lives of converts to Christianity, many of whom were slaves. Paul's message is about making God the true Lord of one's life. Regardless of circumstances or station in life, Paul's admonition is for the individual to expend every ounce of energy as though for God. He is effectively saying to take ownership of one's own motives and to not be defeated or subverted by life's circumstances and to let the great commandment manifest itself at all times. This is a powerful and empowering message. It is the same as Jesus' admonition in the Sermon on the Mount. Matthew 5:39-41 reads in part "If anyone strikes you on the right cheek, turn the other also; and if anyone wants to suc you and take your coat, give your cloak as well; and if anyone forces you to go one mile, go also the second mile."

Jesus is not upholding abusers in this passage. To turn the other cheek, to give the cloak also, to go the extra mile is to provide radical witness to those who would be enemies. It is to risk gaining the attention of others in such a way that they too might be won to Christ. When Jesus says, "Take up your cross and follow me," he is inviting each of us to enter a new kind of landscape. First, we realize our freedom in him. We no longer do the expected or take the easiest road. We confront others with the love of God. We destroy enemies by turning them into friends. For those whose hearts will not be changed, we at least begin by demonstrating to them on some level, the limitations of their coercive power over us.

As related in the short epistle to Philemon, Paul's clear expectation in the case of the slave, Onesimus, is that the master would be moved by righteousness to free him. For, indeed, how does one enslave a brother? Do we regard Joseph's brothers as righteous when they sell their sibling into slavery? The fact is that we vigorously protest this treatment. We see, however, in Genesis 37-47, as the story of Joseph and his brothers unfolds, that God takes what was meant for evil and makes something good occur. It is demonstrated to us in their story that recognition of sin, obedience to God, contrition, forgiveness, and total reconciliation are possible.

This is Paul's message too. Again and again Paul adjures the believers to love one another. He emphasizes that we are all one in Christ and that in him there is no slave or free, male or female, Greek or Jew. To be one in Christ is an all-or-nothing proposition. When he adjures masters to treat their slaves fairly, there is only one ultimate outcome. One cannot love and enslave at the same time. No matter how benign or cruel its appearance, slavery is always rooted in conflict and enmity. When is it not? Paul's way of dealing with the question is one of ultimate unity.

Given that it was in fact instituted, if American slavery had been subject to Pauline disciplines, not one child would have been sold away from one mother, not one husband would have been separated from one wife, not one cruel abusive act could have been justified, and the institution would have fallen away in short order, as it was held before the mirror of brotherly love. To treat a slave fairly is to recognize the dignity of labor and to realize that the laborer is worthy of his hire. He is not a thing, but a man with marvelous capacities. He is worthy. His labor, his person, and his thoughts belong to him and to God. To enslave persons and to serve God are incompatible, as one cannot enslave the image of Christ and yet serve and worship God in truth.

When one totally capitulates to God's power, one can stand on Scripture and understand oneself and all others as being created in the image of God. This is to be empowered to demand in love for oneself and others, the birthright of a child of God.

This was the foundation of the quest for freedom and self-understanding that the African American slaves embraced. So the demand for freedom is meant as a gift for all and is one through which all benefit.

We know that personal freedom was a long time coming for Black people in the American South as it was for the Jews exiled in Egypt. In each case, the people as a whole did not lose their inner lives in large part because they had a sense of belonging to God. Even if nobody else knew their troubles, God did. African Americans understood that Jesus was able to sympathize with their weakness, and had been tested even further than they had. It was not lost on them that this Innocent One was betrayed and reviled and whipped and scorned and mercilessly crucified and yet rose to glory for our sake. Slaves intimately understood that Jesus was truly one of us in the most personal sense.

Nobody Knows the Trouble I've Seen
Nobody knows the trouble I've seen,
Nobody knows but Jesus;
Nobody knows the trouble I've seen,
Glory Hallelujah.

Sometimes I'm up, sometimes I'm down,
Oh, yes, Lord.
Sometimes I'm almost to the ground,
Oh! Yes, Lord.
Oh, Nobody knows the trouble I've seen,
Nobody knows my sorrow,
Nobody knows the trouble I've seen,
Glory Hallelujah.

The slave thought, "If Jesus knows my trouble, I am saved. Though I be slave or free, if I can call Jesus friend, I am saved and can still shout, 'Glory!'" In 1819, Russian poet, Alexander Pushkin, wrote of what he termed a "mysterious freedom" in the lines of the poem of the long title, "In Response to the Challenge to Compose Verses in Honour of H.M. Elisaveta Alexeevna":

Love and a mysterious freedom
Taught my heart a simple hymn.

This same mysterious inner freedom, rooted in love, was apparent enough to the enslaved to permit them to sing and to hold on to hope and to maintain an inner life of faith and resilience. They developed a conviction that there is a source so deep it cannot be measured, and a love so true it cannot die, a God so present he cannot be forgotten, and a truth stronger than strength. Oh, freedom. No matter what twisted logic, no matter what cruel treatment, no matter what deceits were employed, the very facts of the gifts of life and thought contradicted the impositions of slavery.

Give Me Jesus
Oh, when I come to die,
Oh, when I come to die,
When I come to die,
Give me Jesus.
Give me Jesus,
Give me Jesus,
You can have all the world,
Give me Jesus.

And when I am alone,
When I am alone,
When I am alone,
Give me Jesus.
Give me Jesus,
Give me Jesus,
You can have all the world,
Give me Jesus.

"Give Me Jesus" is a total acceptance of the truth Jesus reveals in his declaration: "I am the way, the truth, and the life." This truth of which he speaks has the power to awaken us to freedom. Through himself, Christ offers us the freedom of the truth. His truth allows us to surrender to grace, to understand who our Lord is. It leads us to the realization that our God wishes to be united with us and that he is an ever-present help in this world and the next. Truth is a weapon against fear, deceit, temptation, and exploitation. It is a bulwark against troubles. The lyrics to "Give Me Jesus" are a proclamation that I have found my savior, I have found my justification, I have found my home, I have found the truth, I have found an ultimate way to be free.

In his words on the same theme, there is a deliberate combination of two profound realities in Jesus' promise, "If you continue in my word, you are truly my disciples, and you will know the truth and the truth will make you free" (John 8:31-32). Jesus is speaking of an ultimate freedom, not a freedom in a far-distant future, but an accessible freedom that is integrally dependent on truth. It is an inner freedom, out of which grows the courage to live as a free being. This inner freedom, provided by knowing the truth, is infinitely more important than the appearance of outward freedom. Grasping what is meant by a freedom based in truth is essential to understand what theologian Paul Tillich referred to as the ground of being. In his seminal book, *The Courage to Be,* Tillich speaks of the dread of non-being, not meaning a fear of death, but more a fear of meaninglessness. For Tillich, true self-affirmation can become realized when one wrestles with ultimate concerns of what it means "to be." For Tillich, God does not "exist" as such, but is the very essence of being, and therefore is the ground of our being. This is not an atheistic point of view, but one that points us in the direction of the infinite and our participation in God and in his truth. Knowing the truth makes one free to be in full communion with the spirit of God and provides a basis to treat others as full human beings. Can we state such a truth adequately? No, but we can live such a truth as God has enabled us. The song "Give Me Jesus" recognizes what the freeing power of the Lordship of Jesus, the Christ, means for an individual's life, no matter the circumstances of that life. People in slavery grasped this idea.

These people of faith saw what the sociologist misses about being grounded in faith. To view the church simply as a human institution, duty bound to promote social ideals, is to miss the essence of participation in the body of Christ and the call to discipleship. Seeking social change and social justice are the by-products of living the law of love. First, we seek the kingdom of God. Wisdom, justice, mercy, and the fruits of the love are then the products of being gripped by the Spirit and abiding in truth and love.

I submit that, rather than being duped into accepting twisted scriptural teachings and having "the white man's god" foisted upon them, what happened among illiterate enslaved people in the American South is exactly what Christ promised in John 14:16-17:

And I will pray the Father, and he will give you another Counselor, to be with you forever, even the Spirit of truth, whom the world cannot receive, because it neither sees him nor knows him; you know him, for he dwells with you, and will be in you. (RSV)

Spirit does mean God is present. The enslaved people, hearing the gospel, believed, as recorded in John 16:13: "When the spirit of truth comes, he will guide you into all the truth."

Having been stripped of dignity and justice, yet being armed with the truth of their birthrights as human beings, and assured of the unfailing fellowship of Christ himself, African Americans nurtured the spiritual fortitude to seek social freedom as well as the mysterious inner freedom that all persons can come to know. Like the psalmist, each person who hears and responds to the Word can declare:

Even though I walk through the valley in the shadow
    of death,
I fear no evil; for thou art with me.
—Psalm 23:4, RSV

Claims to Fellowship

Some of the most moving and familiar spirituals are those having to do with personal devotion. Songs about the individual heart that is moved to claim fellowship with God can speak directly to us all. Clearly, individual slaves found succor and strength in binding themselves to Christ. They discovered for themselves the newness of life that Christ offers. They expressed their devotion, contrition, hopes, and failures in song. "Steal Away" is a song that some people believe was used as a signal or mask song to covertly communicate an opportunity to actually escape from slavery. Mask songs were intended to fool those in authority and perhaps allow a person to connect with someone from the underground railroad. "Steal Away" very likely served this purpose on occasion, but it certainly also had true and deep meaning as a devotional song and is based on biblical texts.

Steal Away

Steal away, steal away

Steal away to Jesus.

Steal away, steal away home.

I ain't got long to stay here.

My Lord, he calls me,

He calls me by thunder.

The trumpet sounds within a' my soul.

I ain't got long to stay here.

Green trees a' bending.

Poor sinner stands a' tremblin"

The trumpet sounds within a' my soul.

I ain't got long to stay here.

God's voice as thunder and the trumpet call as a signal to action are common images throughout the Old Testament, but this song text appears to be based on the book of Revelation. Nevertheless, "Steal Away" does not deal with the end of the world so much as the end of the individual's earthly life, despite the fact that the "green trees a bending" image is from Revelation. Chapter 9:4 reads: "they were told not to harm the grass of the earth or any green growth or any tree" (RSV). This is at the sound of the fifth trumpet. The lyricist has married apocalyptic imagery to the hope that those saved in Christ go directly to him when called home by the trumpet. In the meantime, one can steal away to Jesus in quiet prayer at any moment. "Steal Away" is powerful in these representations.

Another song that centers on the individual relationship with God is "This Little Light of Mine." Popular as a Sunday school song, this is a simple commitment to living a life of service, humility, and obedience to the word of God. It is a claim that personal integrity matters. There are many biblical texts regarding light, but Matthew 5:14-16 is the special text from which the song is derived. It reads, "You are the light of the world. A city built on a hill cannot be hidden. No one after lighting a lamp puts it under a bushel basket, but on the lampstand, and it gives light to all in the house. In the same way, let your light shine before others, so that they may see your good works and give glory to your Father in heaven."

"This Little Light of Mine" is one of many examples of the slaves building upon a favorite verse and setting it to music. This made the verse easy to remember and available to share with others.

This Little Light of Mine

This little light of mine,

I'm goin' to let it shine.

This little light of mine,

I'm goin' to let it shine.

This little light of mine,

I'm goin' to let it shine.

Let it shine, let it shine, let it shine.

Everywhere I go,

I'm goin' to let it shine.

Everywhere I go,

I'm goin' to let it shine.

Everywhere I go,

I'm goin' to let it shine.

Let it shine, let it shine, let it shine.

Hide it under a bushel? No!

I'm goin' to let it shine.

Hide it under a bushel? No!

I'm goin' to let it shine.

Let it shine let it shine, let it shine.

"Lord, I Want to Be a Christian" is a well-known song that has made its way into many hymnals. In singing "I want to be a Christian in my heart; I want to be more loving; I want to be more holy; I want to be like Jesus in my heart," a plea is extended, asking God to make of the individual what he intended humanity to be. It is a plea to be made and molded in accordance with the will of God, to be transformed from the inside.

Among ourselves, African Americans often comment that we can testify to something about God and our faith. We testify! Someone testified and set to song, "I want to be a Christian." What does that mean? It is to say that I am one who has heard the good news. It is to be one who has been transformed and made new. It is to be one who listens with the ears of discernment and compassion. It is to be one who sees with the eyes of faith. It is to be one who walks in grace and gratitude. It is to be one caught in the grips of an unending love. It is to be one who knows forgiveness and who forgives over and over again. It is to be one who humbly seeks the companionship of the Lord. It is to be one at whose center is a strong core of joy. It is to bear life's crosses strengthened by Christ himself. And with all of these things, it is to be one whose actions are done as if for God. Someone whom the world considered as a mere slave knew a different reality, and decided and then testified, "Lord, I want to be a Christian."

Personal holiness was clearly a desire of the heart for slaves who became Christians and they composed compelling songs to share these longings with others. Very many songs fit this category. Among them are "I Want to Be Ready," "Lord, Until I Reach My Home," "O, My Good Lord, Show Me the Way" and "Give Me Jesus." These are rich meditative pieces that foster moments of deep reflection for anyone seeking a closer walk with God. These are songs of action and preparation. These are songs about living life, not just existing according to the dictates of others. These are the songs of a thinking people and a people of vision.

Calls to Repentance

Some spirituals were composed as calls to repentance. Solemn warnings of divine retribution, of devastation and final destruction, and of pursuit by the powers of evil resound as themes in these particular songs. Such warnings are always couched in love. Sharing the hope for salvation is the predominant element in these songs. "Sinner Please Don't Let Dis Harvest Pass," "Somebody's Knocking at Your Door" "Hush, Hush, Somebody's Calling My Name," "I Got a Home in-a Dat Rock," "My Lord Says He's Goin' to Rain Down Fire," and "Elijah, Rock" are few examples in which this calling others to repentance is a marvelous sign of caring. The word *please* is drawn out to great effect in the singing of "Sinner, Please Don't Let Dis Harvest Pass." It is an attention-getting supplication, preceding an image taken from Scripture that equates the saving of souls with harvesting. Sometimes, what has been referred to as the childlike simplicity of spirituals, is just as often an effective economy of words that serves to emphasize one particular point. There is not one wasted word in the refrain of this song. The message is unmistakable. We are all sinners, and we all have been offered the gift of salvation. Only our own foolish obstinacy, blindness, rejection, and hardness of heart can rob us of this gift. "Don't die and lose yo' soul at last . . ." the slaves sang to one another in doleful tones.

Sinner, Please Don't Let Dis Harvest Pass

Sinner, please don't let dis harvest pass.
Sinner, please don't let dis harvest pass.
Sinner, please don't let dis harvest pass.
And die and lose yo' soul at last.
I know that my redeemer lives.
I know that my redeemer lives.
I know that my redeemer lives.
Sinner, please don't let dis harvest pass.
My God is a mighty man of war.
My God is a mighty man of war.
My God is a mighty man of war.
Sinner, please don't let dis harvest pass.

By contrast, "Elijah, Rock" is a lively song that is primarily an exhortation to avoid temptations and the wiles of the devil.

The words in one passage are "Satan's a liar and a conjurer, too. If you don't watch out, he'll conjure you." Both Moses and Elijah are mentioned in the song. The idea is to be like them, standing firmly grounded on the same rock of faith. We are to learn not only from the words, but from the examples of Moses and Elijah. "If I could, I surely would just stand on the rock where Moses stood."

The liveliness of spirituals like this and "I Got a Home in-a Dat Rock" imparts a sense of fun and enjoyment, a desired feature of camp meetings. The playful character of the music, however, was never meant to detract from the seriousness of the message. The interweaving of colorful, dramatic story, upbeat rhythms, and folk melody is highly effective in driving home the point in these songs, especially to children and young people whom the songs were intended to teach and fortify.

"I Got Home in-a Dat Rock" is a song of witness and assurance as well as a call to repentance. It incorporates the Old Testament story of Noah and the New Testament story of the poor man, Lazarus, to make the point that we will all be called to accountability. The unsophisticated language of the song text is able to stand alone in conveying clear lessons on witness, assurance, and the need for repentance.

I Got a Home in-a Dat Rock

I got a home in-a dat rock, don't you see?

I got a home in-a dat rock, don't you see?

Between de earth an' sky, thought I heard my Savior cry:

You got a home in-a dat rock, don't you see?

Po' man Laz'rus, po' as I, don't you see?

Po' man Laz'rus, po' as I, don't you see?

Po' man Laz'rus, po' as I,

When he died he foun' a home on high.

He had a home in-a dat rock, don't you see?

Rich man dives, he lived so well, don't you see?

Rich man dives, he lived so well, don't you see?

Rich man dives, he lived so well,

When he died, he foun' a home in hell.

He had no home in-a dat rock, don't you see?

God gave Noah de rainbow sign, don't you see?

God gave Noah de rainbow sign, don't you see?

God gave Noah de rainbow sign,

No mo' water but fiah next time.

Better get a home in-a dat rock, don't you see?

Don't you see that the power of Scripture is not dependent upon the literacy of the hearers or on the ability to speak in flawless language? Simply stated, unembellished truths shared among believers reflect the blessing and sanctity of God. It is the truth that matters.

Images of Grace

The Jordan River Valley is the site of Moses' burial and of Elijah's ascension into heaven by chariot. The Jordan River is not especially impressive as rivers go. It isn't the Mississippi or the Nile or even the Susquehanna. It is not mighty or raging or deep or wide. Its power lies in its holiness and its place in history. Joshua divided the Jordan River for the Israelites to cross into Canaan. Moses was permitted to view the promised land from over the Jordan River, and John's ministry as the forerunner of Jesus involved baptizing many repentant converts in this holy site. There is something about the Jordan River that represents the edge of promise and engenders strong beliefs that we are about to cross over to something better.

This river figures prominently in a number of African American spirituals. It is revered as the site of Jesus' baptism, and is sung of both metaphorically and literally. Songs like "Stan' Still, Jordan," "Deep River," "Roll, Jordan, Roll," and "Wasn't That a Wide River" all evoke images of a chilly, cold, formidable force that separates us from our natural home in heaven (which is also a dominant theme in many spirituals). At the same time, such songs suggest the constantly moving currents and uncertainties of life here on earth and the creative power of God that is displayed in nature as well as the holy waters of baptism.

There is a majesty in the song "Stan' Still, Jordan" that brings one right to the banks of the river. The melody is like the flow of the waters of a river, and the passionate hope and joy that shine through the lyrics are as moving as being at the water's edge. "Stan' Still, Jordan . . . Lord, I can't stan' still . . ." I can't stand still, any more than a river can stand still because my soul is so full. I am so full of the promises of the joys that await me in heaven that I am compelled to sing praises. Earthly concerns might chill my body like the cold, wild waters of a river, but nothing can chill my soul. I belong to God! This is the central message of "Stan' Still, Jordan." It is a message to be shared. It is a message that transcends time and circumstance and the artificial barriers of skin color and social station. I belong to God and must celebrate this fact.

The hope that others may be moved to celebrate communion with God is implicit in a great many spirituals. In "Deep River," with it's rich imagery, the question is asked:

Oh, don't you want to go
To that gospel feast,
That promised land,
Where all is peace?

These images . . . "a gospel feast . . . a promised land . . . peace" . . . take us past the metaphor of the river as the cycle of life. They take us to the heavenly realms where a feast for the soul is prepared and where one's deepest longings are fulfilled. They take us to a promised land where mercy and justice and peace abide and prevail. These are not unsophisticated concepts. These are not reflections of a people happy in bondage who have appropriated their oppressor's view of the unworthiness of the slave. These are the entrenched beliefs of a people who claim as the truth that they too are among the beloved. These are the beliefs of a people whose lives on earth are troubled, but who hold fast to the belief that life on earth is not all that there is.

Just what must a gospel feast be? I believe that it is the fulfillment of 1 Corinthians 13:12: "Now we see through a glass, darkly; then we shall see face to face: now I know in part; but then I shall know even as I am known" (KJV). A gospel feast is the occasion for being fed on the word of God in all its pristine clarity; an occasion where no one can mistake God's meanings and intentions; an occasion for aligning our wills perfectly with God's so that all is made right; an occasion where there is no enmity and hatred; an occasion of unsurpassed peace.

The question, "Don't you want to go to that gospel feast?" is an invitation to others to seek the joys of heaven. This is an effort at sharing the good news. This invitation to salvation, to wholeness, is repeated in the theme of "Roll, Jordan, Roll." The sweet sounds of the living waters of the river will soothe the soul at last in the heavenly places. At last, one will experience the holiness that the earthly river had merely foreshadowed. In paradise at last, one can be joined by others in the kingdom of God, and enjoy the gifts of the spirit eternally. The sounds of the holy river are the accompaniment to everlasting peace and blessed fellowship.

"Wasn't That a Wide River" reflects a different mood. It clearly depicts the Jordan River as symbolizing all of the events, good and bad, in an individual's life, and the final event, death. In this song, the idea of how one is tempted and threatened by Satan is offset by how one manages to persevere due to the grace of God. On the other side of the river, however, there is heaven.

Wasn't That a Wide River

Wasn't that a wide river,

Oh, wasn't that a wide river?

River of the Jordan, Lord?

Wide river,

There's one more river to cross.

Oh, the river of Jordan is so wide,

One more river to cross.

I don't know how to get on the other side,

One more river to cross.

I have some friends before me gone,

One more river to cross.

By the grace of God I'll follow on,

One more river to cross.

Shout, shout, Satan's about,

One more river to cross.

Shut your door and keep him out,

One more river to cross.

Ol' Satan is like a snake in the grass,

One more river to cross.

If you don't mind he'll get you at last,

One more river to cross.

Even in its simplicity, this song helps to belie the notion that the religious thinking of the slaves was wholly derivative rather than inspired. The central message of this song is of the sufficiency of God's grace. Grace is not a concept that is easy to internalize, and yet the expectation of salvation through grace is apparent. Grace is God giving himself to man. We can think of grace as an essential component of the loving nature of God that he extends toward his creation. God is a giver. The slave understood that, through no effort of his own but by the grace of God, he could join those who have gone on before. Despite all efforts to separate us from our creator, there is a mercy seat. Despite the bitterness of the journey across the Atlantic, it remains true:

> Many waters cannot quench love,
> Neither can the floods drown it.
> —Song of Songs 8:7

Lyrics of Hope

Like the ancient Israelites, the African American slaves longed for peace, freedom, and justice in the here and now, but they also envisioned an ultimate promised land. There was heaven on the other side of the deep, wide, dangerous life-sustaining river. This emphasis on the other world had a dual purpose: to give voice to their beliefs and hopes about heaven and the transformative power of God, and to articulate some social ideals to strive for in this present life. Implicit in ideas of how things will be in heaven are ideas of how things ought to be on earth. In heaven, things will be right. In heaven, things will be as they should be, as God intended. In heaven, relationships will be godly, and all the needs of glorious existence will be met. Sorrows will end, and joy abound.

"Ain't Dat Good News" and "I Got a Robe" address simple needs and wants. It is easy to imagine these songs being jointly composed in fields as work songs, and the musical conversation taking place as people added their wants to the list of possessions that may be had in heaven. Things like shoes and decent clothing were basic needs often denied to the enslaved. These were things to be desired. Wings and harps may convey naïveté, but they capture an essential truth about a life given over to God. They imply being changed and made new. "Ain't Dat Good News" sometimes concludes with the verse, "I got a savior in a-dat kingdom." The best news is the last news in this song. The song builds toward the real treasure in heaven.

In "I Got a Robe," along with hopes and dreams about heaven, is the recurring warning that "Everybody talkin' 'bout heaven ain't a-goin' there." This is significant in its implications for accountability. Here is the idea that God will judge. Here too is evidence that refutes the suggestion of E. Franklin Frazier in *The Negro Church in America* that the slaves viewed God as little more than a kindly version of a benevolent plantation master. Certainly much of what was known about the Bible came from the slave holders themselves, but the slaves listened with discernment. "Everybody talkin' 'bout heaven ain't a goin' there" meant that those talking the talk, but not walking the walk might well find themselves numbered among the goats rather than the sheep. God's requirements to do justice, love mercy, and walk humbly with him was understood as uncompromising and meant for everyone. The lessons of the biblical prophets were taken seriously by the slaves.

Differing in mood from the two songs above is "A City Called Heaven." It is more than anything else a plaintive cry against the pain of individual loneliness. It exposes the problem and reality of human suffering with great poignancy. There is a longing for release from this world and its suffering and uncertainty. It is ultimately a song of decision and a song of hope, but certainly sung by one deeply wounded and crying out to God.

A City Called Heaven

I am a poor pilgrim of sorrow,
I've come to this great land alone,
I've heard of a city called heaven,
And I've started to make heaven my home.
Sometimes I'm torn and driven,
Sometimes I don't know which way to roam,
But I've heard of a city called heaven,
And I've started to make heaven my home.
My mother has reached that pure glory,
My father's still walking in sin,
My brothers and sisters don't own me,
'Cause I'm trying to make it on in.

It is an important song because of the individual angst that it captures. Just like anyone else, the individual enslaved person needed to arrive at a sense of self-understanding and come to terms with life beyond the contexts of family, beyond the contexts of community, beyond the expectations of others, and even beyond place and station in life. There was a need to make an inner commitment to believe in an ultimate reality and to act in accord with such beliefs. The composer of this song confesses to uncertainty about the road to heaven and about the weight of heavy concerns. The words tell of real losses, both through death and through alienation from others, and yet of the volitional choice to seek heaven no matter the costs. When Lutheran theologian Dietrich Bonhoeffer wrote of the cost of discipleship, he echoed the same refrain: grace is sufficient, yet in claiming a home in heaven, in claiming Jesus as Lord, there is also an urgent call to action. We live out and act out our faith regardless of the price, because we are compelled to do so. Bonhoeffer's poem, "Who Am I?" written from prison where the evil forces of the Nazi regime had placed him, could so well be juxtaposed with the reflections presented in "A City Called Heaven," written from a prison called slavery.

"Soon-a Will Be Done" is a spiritual in a similar vein. It acknowledges that the troubles in this world are heavy. Still, there is hope and purpose. There is a place of surcease from sorrow; a place of reunion with loved ones; a heavenly home where a savior awaits.

Certainly among the great songs reflecting on loneliness is "Sometimes I Feel Like a Motherless Child." The loneliness spoken of in this song is not necessarily a product of enslavement, notwithstanding the fact that being separated from one's ancestral homeland does equate strongly with the loss of a mother. This kind of lament is one that anyone might feel a need to voice at some point in life. The feeling of being terribly disconnected from one's fellows is a common human experience. To be a little child, alone and a long way from home, would be daunting indeed. The notion of home is the comfort underlying this song.

A song that incorporates a more definite hope and focus for this present life and that attempts to address the question of suffering is "There Is a Balm in Gilead": "There is a balm in Gilead to heal the sin-sick soul and to make the wounded whole." This declaration is a crystallization of God's saving grace. The root word of salvation is *salus,* meaning health and wholeness. Salvation is the promise of restoration to spiritual health and wholeness, to conforming to God's original intent and purpose. In this African American folk hymn is the recognition of the ultimate need for healing from sin and injury caused by sin. Here I mean sin in a large sense, as a pervading force underlying large scale rebellion against the will of God. There is a recognition in "There Is a Balm in Gilead" that human suffering is rooted in sin and is against the plan of God. There is the recognition that broken and distorted relationships, the misuse and abuse of power, our failure to regard each other as members of the same family of God, and our failures to pursue justice, mercy, and ethical living for everyone are the results of such sin. Gilead, more than representing heaven as a place, represents a state of grace. Gilead symbolizes God's redemptive, healing love. "There Is a Balm in Gilead" reveals much about how the slaves viewed man and God. It is a song about revival of the spirit. It is a song about being lifted up from despair and finding strength through Christ to use our poor gifts to share the good news that "he died to save us all." The view of God that emerges from songs such as this is as One uniquely able to transform lives. He is able to plumb the hearts and minds of all and to heal and redeem. He is able to receive the poorest gifts and turn them into treasures. He is able to restore and unite his people.

There Is a Balm in Gilead

There is a balm in Gilead
To make the wounded whole.
There is a balm in Gilead
To heal the sin-sick soul.
Sometimes I feel discouraged
And think my works in vain.
But then the Holy Spirit
Revives my soul again.
If you cannot preach like Peter,
If you cannot pray like Paul,
You can tell the love of Jesus,
And say "He died for all."

Is there no balm in Gilead? Is there no physician there? Why then has the health of my poor people not been restored?
—Jeremiah 8:22

Go up to Gilead, and take balm, O virgin daughter Egypt! In vain you have used many medicines; there is no healing for you.

—Jeremiah 46:11

Clearly the composers of the spiritual, "There Is a Balm in Gilead" were moved by these Jeremiah texts to lament along with the prophet over the state of God's people, but they were also moved to recognize in the life, death, and resurrection of Jesus the cure for all sin.

There are some songs about heaven that focus on the celebratory nature of that state of grace. "Rock in Jerusalem," "I Got a Home in-a Dat Rock," "Oh Peter, Go Ring Dem Bells," and "Rock My Soul in the Bosom of Abraham" fit this category. These are songs which anticipate that biblical personages, such as Abraham, Mary, Martha, and Peter, are waiting to be joined by others from the family of God, and that they, along with the angels, rejoice to receive each of the saved.

In these songs, the saints who have long passed are addressed as though they are available and busy working for the kingdom and listening on the other side of the veil. Some words to "Rock in Jerusalem" are:

Rock in Jerusalem

Oh Mary, Oh Martha,
Oh, Mary, ring dem bells
Oh Mary, Oh Martha,
Oh Mary ring dem bells.
I hear archangels,
They rock in Jerusalem
I hear archangels,
A ringin' dem bells.

The common theme that ties all of these songs together is hope. How do people immersed in conspicuous suffering manage to celebrate in hope? I believe that it is as Paul writes in Romans 8:38-39: "For I am sure that neither death, nor life, nor angels, nor principalities, nor things present, nor things to come, nor powers, nor height, nor depth, nor anything else in all creation, will be able to separate us from the love of God in Christ Jesus our Lord" (RSV). When Christ convicts the heart, there is a light and a hope that sustain.

Witness!

I have a young friend who is suffering from brain cancer. Five surgeries and the effects of radiation and chemotherapy have left his body weak and ravaged and he is unable right now to swallow or speak. Paul is only fifteen, but he is a man in terms of his faith and witness. His light shines all of the time. He lives a life of love. Even in a semiconscious state, in the hours following his surgeries, he would squeeze my hand at the name of Jesus.

It is difficult to know what to say to someone who is so physically incapacitated. How do you have a meaningful visit or anticipate the inner needs of someone so stricken? How do you face your own discomfort at the sight of so many tubes and gauges, and at such helplessness and utter dependency?

When I did not know what to say, I would just sing to Paul. It was possible to watch the effects registering on his heart monitor and breathing apparatus as his spirit calmed while he listened to the songs. All indications were that his body's functions settled into very acceptable ranges. "Steal Away," "Swing Low Sweet

Chariot," and "Kumbayah" must have had deep meaning for him. I believe, however, that it was more than the words or the melodies or the sound of my familiar voice that relieved his agitation. For both of us, God was very present in these moments. These were holy moments beside the bed of this young boy in intensive care. They were moments of grace and light. I believe so strongly that we bring God to each other in love, and that God meets us in all of our efforts.

Paul's suffering is the type of conspicuous suffering that calls faith into question for many people. What can we say about a God who allows such things? Sickness, disease, distress, injustice, unfulfilled lives, and all manner of suffering and anguish do exist. There is a reality and a horror to suffering that we all decry. There is indeed evil in this world. How do we avoid blaming God, our creator, for these evil things? How can God allow such awful conditions to exist? Jesus himself cried out from the cross in anguish at his sense of being forsaken, left alone, in the midst of great pain and torment. This is Jesus! Suffering is real and problematic.

It is not possible for anyone with even a modicum of compassion to look on suffering and not be moved, to not be at once repelled by the suffering and drawn to the sufferer. Is God so different? Are we forsaken? This is our deepest fear. Beyond even the pain of suffering is the desperate thought that God has turned from us. We fear that we have been separated from God. Even for the innocent, even for Jesus, the experience of this despair is not foreign. The fundamental meaning of despair is the belief that God himself has left us, and we are utterly alone and beyond hope.

The Bible speaks of the powers and principalities that rule this world. We are to understand that there is that part of creation that is in rebellion against God, against God's love, against God's will, against God's creative purposes. These are the powers that work to separate us from divine love and will and from each other. These things are the roots of evil and underlie suffering. We do live in a world that has good and bad aspects. But we also live in a world where there is the power of God to transform even what is evil. We are challenged in this life not to accept evil, but to fight the good fight against it. The great commandment to love our neighbors as ourselves is surely manifest in our medicines, our technologies, our peace conferences, our research, our prayers, and our good will toward others.

God does not will evil. God's will for each of us is salvation and atonement, that is, wholeness and at "one"-ment with him.

God is available to us always, despite the occurrence of evil in our lives. Paul Tillich's sermon on principalities and powers in his book, *The New Being,* sheds a wondrous light on the problem of suffering. I highly recommend reading this sermon for those who question how the sufferer can celebrate God in his or her life. I do understand why my forebears who were slaves, and why a young man like my friend Paul, can bear the light for Christ even in the devastations of their acute suffering. There is a God who loves. God's love is so redemptive and complete that nothing created can utterly darken it or conquer it. When we meet God in our suffering, we can allow him to draw good even from the midst of terrible trouble. God is able. The triumph of Christ through his obedience, suffering, and death was a final triumph. Many Christians understand this and are able to persevere in faith in spite of the trials of life.

It will never be my intention at any time to dismiss or gloss over suffering. I can hardly read Elie Wiesel's accounts of the deaths in concentration camps of his beloved mother and father and his little sister, Tzipora, without weeping afresh each time. I abhor suffering, but I believe in God in spite of suffering. I will never say to a sufferer, "It is God's will." I consider this insulting both to God and the sufferer. Somehow or the other, however, I suspect that the possibility of suffering is a necessary condition for freedom. For us to have the gift of possibilities—and therefore real freedom—one possibility we must both allow for and endure is the possibility of suffering. Importantly, we are given ways to try to mitigate this circumstance in that we have the creative power and the duty to attempt to alleviate suffering when we encounter it. Implicit in Christ's command to love one another is recognition of this burden to relieve each other's suffering.

I believe that God is present with us in our suffering, not as the cause, not as a silent, distant, and indifferent witness, not as a merciless judge, but as one who affirms life within us despite the fires of anguish in which we sometimes find ourselves. His compassionate concern for humanity is the basis of our own. As we bear his image in our very being, he bears our trials with us, sometimes transforming us in unexpected ways as we journey through our trials. I believe that God is a creator, a sustainer, and yes, a sufferer right along with each of us, whether fallen sparrow or tragic human victim of a terrible fate. He knows the reality of our tragedies and is in our very tears. Unless this is true, that it is tragic to suffer and die, how can we begin to understand the meaning of the passion and crucifixion of Jesus? We do not need to be ashamed of our tears, nor reluctant to mourn our very real losses, nor hesitant to call on God to be with us from the depths of our griefs. Jesus wept. I am moved and assured by his weeping.

I can say with certain conviction the words of a simple song: "My soul is a witness for my Lord." I stand with Daniel, Mary and Martha, Samson, Methuselah, and the cloud of witnesses who proclaim hope and the good news of salvation. When I sing "My Soul Is a Witness," I am proclaiming that I know suffering and I know failure, but I am loved by the Lord of life. Despite the terrors of the day, there is that in me that clings to the certainty of the absolute goodness of God.

"My Soul Is a Witness" is a joyful proclamation to be sung with passion and delight. It is a celebration of goodness. It is a testament to the timelessness of God's presence among us as it recalls his faithfulness to those who have gone before.

My Soul Is a Witness

My soul is a witness for my Lord,
My soul is a witness for my Lord.
You read in the Bible
And you understand
Methuselah was the oldest man.

He lived nine hundred and sixty-nine,

Then he died and went to heaven, Lord,

In a due time.

Methuselah was a witness for my Lord.

Methuselah was a witness for my Lord.

You read in the Bible

And you understand

Samson was the strongest man.

Samson went out at a one time,

And he killed about a thousand of the Philistine.

Oh Samson was a witness for my Lord,

Oh Samson was a witness for my Lord.

Now Daniel was a Hebrew child.

He went to pray to his God awhile.

The king at once for Daniel did send,

And he put him right down in the lion's den.

God sent his angels,

The lions for to keep,

And Daniel laid down and went to sleep.

Now Daniel was a witness for my Lord,

Daniel was a witness for my Lord.

My soul is a witness for my Lord,

My soul is a witness for my Lord!

These words were indeed written by people in the midst of conspicuous suffering and very conscious of their condition in life, making their witness that much more authentic. In a personal letter to his close friend, Joshua Speed, Abraham Lincoln wrote of captured runaway slaves: "I confess I hate to see the poor creatures hunted down and caught and carried back to their stripes and unrequited toil; but I bite my lips and keep quiet. . . . You may remember as I well do, that from Louisville to the mouth of the Ohio there were on board ten or a dozen slaves shackled together with irons. That sight has continued to torment me, and I see something like it each time I touch the Ohio or any other slave border. It is not fair for you to assume that I have no interest in a thing which has, and continually exercises, the power of making me miserable."

The suffering of others ought to make us miserable, and the more we know Christ, the more acute our misery should be, until we cannot resist the urge to do something about the suffering. Our very souls witness to us about what it is we are compelled to do in this life, and the witness of our souls make us aware from whom our strength and courage to act come.

The Lord is my rock, my fortress, and my deliverer, my God, my rock, in whom I take refuge, my shield, and the horn of my salvation, my stronghold. I call upon the Lord, who is worthy to be praised; so I shall be saved from my enemies.

—Psalm 18:2-3

Sighs Too Deep for Words

Sometimes the holiness of God breaks into our reality in such unexpected, insistent ways, that we are brought to our knees on the spot. It is as if we have our own burning-bush moments where we are struck by the awareness of God's all-encompassing power and majesty and love. In times like these we are compelled to pray. St. Paul tells us that "The Spirit helps us in our weakness; for we do not know how to pray as we ought, but that very Spirit himself intercedes with sighs too deep for words" (Romans 8:26). "Every Time I Feel the Spirit," a very simple slave song, incorporates the truth that something beyond our own selves calls us to the most authentic prayer. Every time I feel the spirit moving in my heart, I will pray with sighs too deep for words.

Prayer is a wonderful and mysterious gift through which we seek communion with God. It is a refuge and a lifeline. It is a hiding place in time of trouble, a sure anchor for life and thought and hope, a channel of pure grace, and a tie that binds humans together. Through prayer we actively seek the will and presence of God and call attention to ourselves. Prayer is talking to God and awaiting his response. In prayer we unveil the longings of the heart, making our needs clear to ourselves as well as bringing them before the holy one. Prayer is our consideration of our state, our place in creation. It is our taking stock of where we are, asking to be made new, to be brought closer to the perfection that God has planned for us. It is asking for divine will to manifest itself in our lives. It is asking to be nurtured in the bosom of God. It is asking to be connected to our source and to be in harmony with the will of our creator. It is also an expression and release of our frustrations and doubts and disappointments. It is not dependent on nor bound by words. We encounter the sacred, and we are empowered through the spirit of God to reach him through prayer. This is the message of "Every Time I feel the Spirit."

So many spirituals are simply prayers set to music. This talking to God from the heart is perhaps the unifying thread for spirituals. "Kumbayah," which means "come by here," is beautiful because of its familiar address and its assurance that all one has to do is ask God to come and be present, and he will. When someone is praying or someone is crying or someone is singing,

God attends. It does not matter who the someone is. It does not matter what the someone says. All that matters is the longing. The Spirit comes with sighs to deep for words, to help us in our need and to be present with us.

Similarly, "I've Been in the Storm So Long" is a recognition that communion with God through prayer is a necessity of life. It conveys the belief that something essential is missing from a life void of prayer. It is an entreaty to be allowed the time for prayer. It is, as the psalmist says, the soul longing and thirsting for God as a hart does for water. Even as the storms of life rage, prayer calms the disquiet of the soul and feeds the fires of the spirit.

"Standin' in the Need of Prayer" is another important song in this vein. It is an acknowledgment of the beam in one's own eye, of sin and failure before God. This idea of personal sin and responsibility was clearly evident among the slaves, and is prominently detailed in a number of spirituals. "Standin' in the Need of Prayer" developed as a song of confession and repentant prayer.

The deep regard for prayer, and a grasp of the rich myriad of approaches to prayer, are clearly demonstrated in the body of African American spirituals that exists. There is a depth to the messages in these songs that is timeless and universal in its reach. "I Couldn't Hear Nobody Pray" is an expression of the need of the uplifting prayers of others. We have a deep need for the prayers of others and are lonely without them.

As a deer longs for flowing streams, so my soul longs for you, O God. My soul thirsts for God, for the living God. When shall I come and behold the face of God?
—Psalm 42:1-2

Gospel Shoes

This poor soul cried and was heard by the Lord, and was saved from every trouble. The angel of the Lord encamps around those who fear him, and delivers them.

—Psalm 34:6-7

As they were leaving Jericho, a large crowd followed him, and suddenly two blind men then sitting by the roadside, who heard that Jesus was passing by, began to shout, "Lord, son of David, have pity on us!" The crowd began to scold them in an effort to reduce them to silence, but they only shouted the louder, "Lord, son of David, have pity on us!" Jesus then stopped and called out to them, "What do you want me to do for you?" "Lord," they told him, "open our eyes!" Moved with compassion, Jesus touched their eyes, and immediately they could see: and they became his followers.

—Matthew 20: 29-34, NAB

As he drew near to Jericho, a blind man was sitting by the roadside begging; and hearing the multitude going by, he inquired what this meant. They told him, "Jesus of Nazareth is passing by." And he cried, "Jesus, Son of David, have mercy on me! And those who were in front rebuked him, telling him to be silent; but he cried out all the more, "Son of David, have mercy on me!" And Jesus stopped, and commanded him to be brought to him; and when he came near, he asked him, "What do you want me to do for you?" He said, "Lord, let me receive my sight." And Jesus said to him, "Receive your sight; your faith has made you well." And immediately he received his sight and followed him, glorifying God.

—Luke 18:35-43, RSV

De Blind Man Stood on the Road and Cried

De blind man stood on de road and cried,
De blind man stood on de road and cried.
Crying, "Oh, my Lord, save me!"
De blind man stood on de road and cried,
Crying that he might receive his sight,
Crying that he might receive his sight,
Crying "Oh, my Lord, save me!"

De blind man stood on the road and cried,

Crying "What kind o' shoes am those you wear?"

Crying "What kind o' shoes am those you wear?"

Crying "Oh, my Lord, save me!"

De blind man stood on de road and cried,

Crying, "Dese shoes I wear am de gospel shoes,"

Crying "Dese shoes I wear am de gospel shoes,"

Crying, "Oh, my Lord, save me."

De blind man stood on de road and cried.

In so many ways we are all like the blind man crying on the road. We cannot see. We cannot find our way alone. We do not know everything that is going on around us. We sense that there is something quite wonderful to be had, and we know that the road we are on leads to somewhere. And so we cry out. We want to go the right way with the right companions. How can we prepare?

We listen carefully, trying to understand what is transpiring around us. We hear testimonies about good and glorious things happening around us. We store up these words like treasures, while hope builds in our hearts. People are coming and going on the road. We are jostled and shuffled and sometimes it is hard to just stay on our feet and not be trampled by the crowd.

Finally we sense someone moving past us with purpose and assuredness and determination. Who could this be? What shoes is he wearing to be so purposeful and directed? We ask and find out that this is someone who knows the Lord Jesus. This is wonderful news. We want to be equipped in the same way, to know this same Lord who saves. We continually cry out, "Save me too, Lord. Save me! Meet me in my needs. Supply my wants. Let me go with you." And he does.

Clad in our own gospel shoes, we joyfully continue on our journey, having been given our sight. We are equipped for service. We cannot always see what is ahead in the road, but we have the assurance that if we follow in the footsteps of the one who leads, we are indeed saved by his power.

That is the message of this old song. This is a creative response to add a sense of immediacy to the stories related in the Bible about God's pity, mercy, and will for us to be whole and have our needs met. It is very typical to find in spirituals that time is often bridged. It is as if we are able to walk right beside the old witnesses from Scripture and observe for ourselves the saving acts that are recounted.

The image of a blind man or of two blind men by the road evokes thoughts of extreme poverty as well as physical disability. The poor blind beggars command Jesus' attention by asking for it, and they receive his compassion. There is little wonder that such hopes would resonate with the enslaved as well. Many things appear to separate the haves from the have-nots; but there is nothing that separates us in our access to God. Poverty of the spirit is not inescapable as sometimes material poverty proves to be. This spiritual helps to illustrate this for us.

Gospel shoes may seem a quaint image, but there is power in such shoes that the rich metaphoric language of the lyrics brings before us. It is in Ephesians 6 that the armor of God is described: the belt of truth; the helmet of salvation; the breastplate of righteousness; the sword of the spirit; the shield of faith; and feet sandaled with the readiness of the gospel of peace. And so we find gospel shoes on the feet of formerly blind beggars who consequently rejoice to follow the Lord. My ancestors very effectively co-opted the language of Scripture in the spiritual "De Blind Man Stood on the Road and Cried" to bring a message of hope to the downtrodden everywhere.

Mary Had a Baby

There is a tender regard for both the baby Jesus and his young mother that is readily apparent in the spirituals "Mary Had a Baby," "The Virgin Mary Had a Baby Boy," and "Sweet Little Jesus Boy." Each of these songs captures the divinity and humanity of Jesus, and they all speak to the mission that he came to accomplish. There is still such a sweetness in these songs when singing of the infant that all his baby softness and warmth and helplessness are poignantly brought before us.

Mary Had a Baby

Mary had a baby,
Sweet lamb,
Mary had a baby,
Sweet lamb,
Mary had a baby,
Mary had a baby,
Mary had a baby,

Sweet lamb.
What did she call him?
Jesus.
What did she call him?
Jesus.
What did she call him?
Called him King Jesus,
Ever lasting Father,
Mighty Prince of Peace.
Mary had a baby,
Sweet lamb.

This is a song that needs to be heard to be fully appreciated. The words are imbued with sensitivity, wonder, compassion, and finally awe for the King of Kings. I especially enjoy what is nearly like a grandmother's cooing over a new mother and baby. This is then tied to the some of the great christological titles for Jesus as the song crescendos. This seamlessness is typical of spirituals. There is no break between the divine and the earthly. Reality is woven of one fabric. This matter-of-fact approach to the objects of faith is one of the beauties of the religious expression that grew from the experience of Africans in America.

The lamb image is prevalent in a number of spirituals. In "Mary Had a Baby," the words are almost breathed in a poignant, reflective sigh. They are at the same time a term of endearment one might use toward any beloved child, and also a recognition that this baby is indeed the holy lamb of God who dies on the cross for all of our sakes. When songs communicate as effectively as this one does, the power of story shines through.

"The Virgin Mary Had a Baby Boy" is another spiritual celebrating the birth of Jesus. It is sung in quiet, clipped, joyful tones. It is a song simply telling who Jesus is, describing his heavenly and earthly origins. The words are:

The Virgin Mary Had a Baby Boy

The virgin Mary had a baby boy.
The virgin Mary had a baby boy.
The virgin Mary had a baby boy,
And they say that his name was Jesus.
He come down, he come from de glory.
He come down, he come from de glorious kingdom.
He come down, he come from de glory.
He come down, he come from de glorious kingdom.

Oh, yes, believer. Oh, yes, believer.
He come from de glory,
He come from de glorious kingdom!

"Sweet Little Jesus Boy" was written in the twentieth century by Robert MacGimsey. In terms of style and focus it fits precisely with spirituals composed in previous eras. It is personal in its address to the Christ child, and even though it takes us through the crucifixion, it is the baby Jesus who remains with us throughout this meditation.

"Go Tell It on the Mountain" and "There's a Star in the East" are great songs celebrating the events of Christmas. These songs are proclamations of majesty. They point us toward the kingship of Christ. These are songs of glory to the newborn king. I am so glad to discover how often these two spirituals are included in hymnals.

Go Tell It on the Mountain
Go tell it on the mountain
Over the hills and everywhere
Go tell it on the mountain
That Jesus Christ is born!

Down in a lowly manger,
The humble Christ was born,
And God sent us salvation
That blessed Christmas morn.

Amen

See the baby,
wrapped in a manger,
on Christmas morning.
Amen. Amen. Amen.
See him in the temple
Talkin' with the elders
Who marveled at his wisdom.
Amen. Amen. Amen.
See him at the Jordan
Where John was baptizin'
And savin' all sinners.
Amen. Amen. Amen.
See him at the seaside
Talkin' to the fishermen
And makin' them disciples.
Amen. Amen. Amen.

Marchin' in Jerusalem
Over palm branches
In pomp and splendor.
Amen. Amen. Amen.
See him in the garden
Prayin' to his Father
In deepest sorrow.
Amen. Amen. Amen.
Led before Pilate
Then they crucified him
But he rose on Easter.
Amen. Amen. Amen.
Hallelujah
He died to save us
And he lives forever.
Amen. Amen. Amen!

The Word made incarnate. God come down to man as a helpless, vulnerable babe born in mean circumstances, come to save the world, come to demonstrate the awesome power of perfect love, come to call us out of darkness into light; breaking into human history to break the chains of sin and death and establish his everlasting kingship so that people of all nations and languages should serve him; come to set us free.

See the baby? See him in the manger? See our God approaching us in the flesh as a tiny newborn baby? See the quaking shepherds, the angel chorus, the wise men traveling from the east? See these holy moments depicted in this song? Stories enable us to see, no matter how far in time we may seem to be removed from an event. They allow our participation and allow our ownership of the embedded meanings.

"Amen" is powerful storytelling. The ancient word *amen* is recognition and affirmation of the holy. In this song, the rhythmic repetition of this word compels the listeners and singers to take time to envision each element of Jesus' life. Each refrain is there to allow us to sharpen our focus on the events brought before us. We claim closer kinship with Jesus in our willingness to see him in these events. It is as if we are there for each of these holy moments.

I love the manner in which "Amen" first depicts a scene from Jesus' life, and then gives time to contemplate that moment. Can you just imagine the rapt attention on the faces of the elders in the temple as they encountered the wisdom of the youthful twelve-year-old Jesus? Can you imagine the pregnant silences, and the excited debates, and the electric atmosphere generated in that place on that day? Amen.

Can you feel the sun shining down on the waters of the Jordan River while John is gathering repentant sinners for baptizing? Can you picture the joy and wonder and fulfillment on John's face when he sees Jesus approaching? Aren't you frozen in awe as the Holy Spirit descends like a dove and the voice of God thunders from the heavens?

Can you smell the sea air when Jesus approaches those fishermen and calls his first disciples? Are you in that crowd in Jerusalem when he makes his triumphal entry? Is your heart heavy as you anxiously and powerlessly wait in the darkness in the garden at Gethsemane and you see his prayerful struggles as he kneels beneath the olive trees?

Is your heart bruised as you see him stand before Pilate?

From our perspective as Easter people, people who know the whole story, we are like the "watchers" in heaven, watching these events unfold time and time again as they are replayed in our minds and spirits. We recall the events of Jesus' earthly life for our own good and in our efforts to share this holy history with others. Our spiritual growth and renewal is fueled by such recollections. "Amen" is an inspired song, full of grace, that makes it as though we were there.

Were You There?

Were you there when they crucified my Lord? This song about the suffering, death, and resurrection of our Lord is perhaps the most beloved and provocative of all African American spirituals. It is a potent reminder every Easter season of the wounds received on our behalf, of the life given up, of the victory over the grave. Through the words of this song, the confines of time evaporate in our encounter with the cross. We are taken to that bleak scene at Golgotha and made to feel the press and hear the shouts of the unsympathetic crowd. We are made to hear the ringing of the hammer, to witness the thirst and the agony, and to shudder at the thrust of the sword. We are brought to our knees and made to weep over the lifeless body of the Lord of Life as he is laid in the tomb. Were you there?

What a question this is. If you were there, what was your capacity? Bystander? Instigator? Rabble rouser? Friend? Protester? Where was your heart in those moments? What became of your hopes? Oddly enough, no one can escape these questions. It does not do to claim "I wasn't even born yet. How could I have been there?" What the slave originators of this song are saying is that all humankind was gathered at the foot of that cross on that day. It was a moment out of time, a moment upon which all human history turns. We all participate in the mystery of those holy days because they were accomplished for us. So, were you there?

Were You There?

Were you there when they crucified my Lord?
Were you there when they nailed him to the tree?
Were you there when they pierced him in his side?
Were you there when the sun refused to shine?
Were you there when they laid him in the tomb?
Were you there when he rose up from the grave?
Refrain:
Oh! Sometimes it causes me to tremble, tremble, tremble.

Oh! Sometimes it causes me to tremble when I go in my mind and spirit to those days. To contemplate this unfathomable demonstration of divine love toward me and toward you leads me into a place of sighs too deep for words. The "Oh!" in the refrain of "Were You There?" is as necessary and compelling and telling as any words ever written. It captures guilt, anguish, love, hope, awe, mystery, and gratitude for the sacrifice made on Calvary. A spiritual beautiful in its interpretation and acceptance of the events of Easter in the plainest language possible, "Were You There?" allows the hours of three days to unfold before us. We can close our eyes and see the savior being nailed to the tree, being pierced in the side, see him die. In the darkness of the hours when the sun refused to shine, what might we have experienced? What might Jesus have experienced lying in the grave? Such questions. When he arose, what then? What since then? What now? "Were you there?" A simple slave song raising simply profound questions.

"Calvary" is a less well-known spiritual written in the same vein as "Were You There?" It is as definite and uncompromising in its proclamation of the events of Easter. It is meditative in its cadence and simplicity. The words are:

Calvary

Refrain:

Calvary, Calvary,

Calvary, Calvary,

Calvary, Calvary.

Surely he died on Calvary.

1. *Every time I think about Jesus,*

Every time I think about Jesus,

Every time I think about Jesus,

Surely he died on Calvary.

2. *Don't you hear the hammer ringing?*

3. *Don't you hear him calling his Father?*

4. *Don't you hear him saying "It is finished?"*

5. *Jesus furnished my salvation*

6. *Sinner, do you love my Jesus?*

The repetition brings the scenes before us and establishes the serious mood. All of the events of the crucifixion are painted for us in bare, stark detail. We are there. We are to understand the reality of these moments for Jesus and for us as real historical moments and as holiest of holy moments. Each time the word *Calvary* is repeated in the refrain, it is imbued with deep remorse and deep gratitude. The sorrow over Christ's suffering resounds as the word *Calvary* is drawn out in this song. Why he suffered is made clear in the verse that proclaims Jesus furnished my salvation. Then, in a commanding verse, we are all asked for decision and declaration. Sinner, do you love my Jesus? "Sinner" is a non-negotiable address, universally applied to us all. Sinner is not an unfriendly address, but a call to recognition of our estate. Sinner, do you love my Jesus? The stark beauty and directness of this song make it one of the most powerful spirituals ever composed.

"Were You There?" and "Calvary" do not stand alone as great spirituals depicting the crucifixion and resurrection of Jesus. There are "He Arose," "He Never Said a Mumbalin' Word," "Jesus Walked That Lonesome Valley," and "Amen." This list is by no means exhaustive, but the number of exclusively Lenten and Easter spirituals is not great. The power to convey the message is formidable in the few compositions that we do have.

I Believe This Is Jesus

I am convinced that the African American slaves and their descendants who embraced Christianity did so at the prompting of the Holy Spirit. The body of sacred folk music that grew out of both the religious experience and the experience of oppression tells the story of a people who found spiritual wealth in the Scriptures. It tells of a God who did not leave his children comfortless and alone. The music reflects an individual and corporate sense of authentic being, of people who know firsthand the joy of the Lord. These people set down the story of their relationship to God in songs that have become timeless. The truths that they discovered for themselves remain undimmed.

Just as people throughout the ages have been inspired by the story of Moses and the Israelites, the suffering and faith of African Americans is recorded in song to inspire others to learn of the God who liberates and vindicates and calls his children to a higher purpose. The mystery of God remains, but his holiness and his goodness and his love for us shine through his approach to us. And so, we sing.

Christians everywhere and in all times have realized that the best thing to do with good news is to share it. The treasure that we have in Jesus is too good to hoard for ourselves. Each person who receives Christ and is given the power to become a child of God is a transformed being eager to worship God in spirit and in truth. There is an urgent joy and a demand from within calling us to discipleship. There is a divine compulsion toward witness as each of us is enabled by the Holy spirit. There is that in us which cries out " I believe . . . I believe this is Jesus! Come and See!" This passionate cry is captured so well in one of my very favorite spirituals.

Like so many spirituals, "I Believe This Is Jesus" is based on several Scriptures which are tied together to great effect in the song. The wonderful refrain is based primarily on two well-known stories recorded in the Gospel of John. These are of Philip and Nathanael and of the Samaritan woman.

In the first case, Philip found Nathanael and said to him, "We have found him about whom Moses in the law and also the prophets wrote, Jesus son of Joseph of Nazareth." Nathanael said to him, "Can anything good come out of Nazareth?" Philip said to him, "Come and see" (John 1:45-46). They encounter Jesus, one with expectation and one with doubt. They are not long in his presence before Nathanael, too, recognizes Jesus as the One. He is convinced and convicted. Philip and Nathanael both devote their lives to Jesus, and invite all to come and see the good that has come out of Nazareth. This joyful experience is well reflected in the song.

Next, in John 4: 7-42, there is Jesus' encounter with the woman at the well in Samaria which is among the most beloved stories in the Bible. Jesus approaches this woman who, due to her questionable past and her status as a lowly Samaritan, is not among the socially powerful. One of the first questions she asks him is why he would ask a Samaritan for water. The gospel writer makes it clear that both parties acknowledge this division between Jews and Samaritans. As always, Jesus is deliberate in choosing exactly the right person to accomplish his purposes.

It is no accident that he chooses a woman, and a fallen woman, and a scorned and oppressed woman, and an intelligent woman, and a woman who has a heart that longs for God, to be his instrument. It is she who is blessed by this pivotal conversation with the Lord, and she who is inspired to exclaim, "Could this be the Christ? Come and see" (John 4:29).

In choosing someone so evidently flawed to be of service to him, Jesus gives us a great gift in the Samaritan woman. Such a model of Christian service fosters and preserves in each of us the hope that we, too, might somehow serve as an instrument of his holy will and purpose, despite our shortcomings or our stations in life. This hope makes us better able to accept the reality of God's acceptance of us just as we are. We are all flawed and not one of us is able to leave the impression that the force and righteousness of our words or actions comes from within us. The completeness of God's power is made manifest when a weak human vessel is filled with God's light, and hope is multiplied.

As we are today, the believers among the enslaved Africans were strengthened by the very weakness of the Samaritan woman, and enjoined to add their voices to hers to share the good news that Christ is present among us . . . and to invite others to come and see the One who has the light of God shining in his eyes and the love of God shining in his face. Come and see this One who tells of mansions in the skies, and of grace and pardon.

I Believe This Is Jesus

I believe this is Jesus.

Come and see, come and see.

Oh, I believe this is Jesus.

Come and see, come and see.

The light of God shines in his face.

Come and see, come and see.

He offers all his pard'ning grace.

Come and see, come and see.

The love of God shines in his eyes.

Come and see, come and see.

He tells of mansions in the skies.

Come and see, come and see.

Did you ever see such love before?

Come and see, come and see.

Saying "Go in peace and sin no more?"

Come and see, come and see.

I am so happy to benefit from the rich musical heritage that my forebears left behind. I am so glad to share in this faith. I, too, believe this is Jesus who leads me and gives me a voice to sing for him. I believe this is Jesus, this holy one who came down from heaven and by the power of the Holy Spirit was made man. I believe this is Jesus, who came to proclaim liberty to the captives, to bind up the brokenhearted, and to bring good news to the afflicted. I believe this is Jesus who is the way, the truth, and the life. I believe this is Jesus of whom the prophets foretold.

I believe this is Jesus who sacrificed his own life for me on Calvary so that I might reach the glorious kingdom. I believe that I shall see the goodness of the Lord in the land of the living!

> *I can say with Job, that I know that my redeemer lives.*
> *I gotta robe and you gotta robe*
> *and all of God's chillun' got a robe.*
> *I believe this is Jesus.*

Wait for the LORD: be strong, and let your heart take courage: wait for the LORD!
—Psalm 27:14

Endnotes

INTRODUCTION

1. Frazier, E. Franklin. *The Negro Church in America* (New York: Schocken Books, 1973).

2. Ibid.

WALKING THE WALK

1. Weil, Simone. *The Iliad or The Poem of Force: A Critical Edition.* James P. Holden, ed. (New York: Peter Lang 2003).

2. Douglass, Frederick. *The Life and Times of Frederick Douglass.* (New York: Pathway Press, 1941).

CD Track List

1. This Little Light of Mine
2. Been in the Storm So Long
3. Hush, Hush
4. Stan' Still Jordan
5. I Want Jesus to Walk with Me
6. Rock in Jerusalem
7. I Got a Robe
8. Let Us Break Bread Together
9. My Soul Is a Witness
10. Oh, Peter, Go Ring Dem Bells
11. Sweet Little Jesus Boy
12. Were You There
13. De Gospel Train
14. I Believe This Is Jesus

Tracks 1–7 are original arrangements by Marsha Hansen and friends. Arr. © 2006 Augsburg Fortress. All rights reserved.

Track 8: Based on the setting found in *Lutheran Book of Worship,* copyright © 1972 Contemporary Worship 4: Hymns for Baptism and Holy Communion. Arr. © 2006 Augsburg Fortress. All rights reserved.

Track 9: Arrangement by H. A. Chambers. From *A Treasury of Negro Spirituals,* Arr. © 1953 Blandford Press, London.

Track 10: Arrangement by Harry T. Burleigh. Copyright © 1984 by Belwin Mills, c/o CPP Belwin, Inc. Miami, FL 33014

Track 11: By Robert MacGimsey. Copyright © 1934 by Carl Fischer, New York.

Track 12: Arrangement by Harry T. Burleigh. Copyright © 1984 by Belwin Mills, c/o CPP Belwin, Inc. Miami, FL 33014

Track 13: Arrangement by Harry T. Burleigh. Copyright © 1984 by Belwin Mills, c/o CPP Belwin, Inc. Miami, FL 33014

Track 14: Arranged by Marsha Hansen. Arr. © 2006 Augsburg Fortress. All rights reserved

CD Credits

Executive Producer: Marsha Hansen

Produced by Rob Fraboni

Engineered by Ben Elliott

Assisted by Mike Schmeider

Recorded at Studio L, Weston, Conn.

Mixed at Showplace Studios, Dover, Conn.

Mastered at Effortless Masters by Craig Dreyer and Mike Schmeider

Sound Engineers in San Diego: Paul Tye and Julian Tydelski at Signature
Sound Studio

Vocals: Marsha Hansen

Backing Vocals: Jordan Hansen, Babi Floyd, Blondie Chaplin, Nick
Tremulis, Walt Gustafson

Guitars: Keith Richards, Nick Tremulis, John Pirruccello, Blondie Chaplin

Pedal Steel Guitar: John Pirruccello

Bass, Viola da Gamba: Paul Nowinski

Piano: Steven Barber, Chuck Leavell, Marsha Hansen, Joyce Perez

Drums and Percussion: George Receli

Keith Richards appears courtesy Virgin Records America, Inc; Rob Fraboni
appears courtesy HandMade Recordings